All About Adoption

Published by
MAGINATION PRESS
An Educational Publishing Foundation Book
American Psychological Association
750 First Street, NE
Washington, DC 20002

For more information about our books, including a complete catalog, please write to us,
call 1-800-374-2721, or visit our website at www.maginationpress.com.

Editor: Darcie Conner Johnston
Art Director: Susan K. White
The text type is Electra
Printed by Phoenix Color, Rockaway, New Jersey

Library of Congress Cataloging-in-Publication Data

Nemiroff, Marc A.
All about adoption : how families are made & how kids feel about it / by Marc Nemiroff
and Jane Annunziata ; illustrated by Carol Koeller.
p. cm.
Summary: Using simple language, describes the stages of the adoption process and discusses
complex feelings commonly felt by adopted children.
ISBN 1-59147-058-7 (cloth : alk. paper) — ISBN 1-59147-059-5 (pbk. : alk. paper)
1. Adoption—Juvenile literature. [1. Adoption.] I. Annunziata, Jane. II. Koeller, Carol, ill.
III. Title.
HV875.N29 2004
362.73'4—dc21   2003007408

Manufactured in the United States of America
10 9 8 7 6 5 4 3 2 1

All About Adoption

How Families Are Made
& How Kids Feel About It

by Marc Nemiroff, Ph.D., and Jane Annunziata, Psy.D.
illustrated by Carol Koeller

MAGINATION PRESS • WASHINGTON, DC

There are lots of different ways to have a baby.

Some parents have one baby.

Some parents have one baby at a time.

And some parents have two or three (or more!) babies all at once.

Babies grow inside a
birth mother.
They have a
birth father too.

Some babies stay with their birth parents
and grow up with them.

Some babies go to new parents and grow up with them. These new parents are called **adoptive parents**.

When you have different parents than your birth parents, it means that you are **adopted**.

Your adoptive parents are your real parents.

They will always love you and take care of you.

All of this is called **adoption**.

So how does adoption start? Adoption has two starts.

Start Number 1
Your birth parents begin to realize that they might
not do a good job taking care of a child.

They think and
think a long time.

And then
they know.

They can't be the
kind of parents that
a child needs.

They wanted you to have everything
a child needs to grow up happy and healthy.

1. Love
2. Attention
3. Good food
4. Feel safe
5. Comfortable home
6. good schools
7. Good doctors
8. Toys and friends to play with

They thought and thought about how
to find the best parents for you.

They knew there were many people
all over the world just waiting for
a child to become part of their family.

That brings us to **Start Number 2**.

Your adoption also started when your adoptive parents wanted a child to love and care for.

They went to someone who could help them find the child for them.

There are lots of different helpers for birth parents and adoptive parents, and they are all over the world.

These helpers are important because adopting a child is so very special.

Some adoption helpers work in something called an **adoption agency**. An adoption agency is a group of people who know a lot about helping children and parents find each other.

Sometimes doctors know how to match adoptive parents with their new children too. Sometimes doctors know parents who want to adopt and children who are ready to be adopted.

And always, lawyers make sure that everything about your adoption is **legal**. That means that all the rules are followed so that your adoption is just right.

The next step is for
the helpers to find out all
about your **birth parents**.
This means the helpers ask lots of questions.
Your birth parents answer the questions,
and they fill out a lot of papers about themselves.

The next step is for
the helpers to find out
all about your **adoptive parents**.
This means the helpers ask lots of questions.
Your adoptive parents answer the questions,
and they fill out a lot of papers about themselves.

Adoption helpers use all of these answers
and papers to find the best parents for you.

Adoption helpers then do a **home study**.
A home study means that your new home was checked out
very carefully by a special adoption helper.

Here is what the helper does:

Meets with the adoptive parents

Meets any other family members living there   Sees your bedroom

Makes sure the
refrigerator has
good food in it!

Looks around the home and neighborhood

Once the home study is finished and the helpers find the right home for you, your adoptive parents start to learn about you.

They read the answers your birth parents gave to the helpers' questions.

If you've already been born, they see pictures of you.

Sometimes they even see a video of you!

They are already getting to know you a little bit.

There is so much to do in the days before your adoptive parents get to meet you.

They get your room ready for you.

They are starting to feel very excited and happy.

They are already starting to fall in love with you.

They can't wait to meet you!

Some parents meet their new children
in the United States.

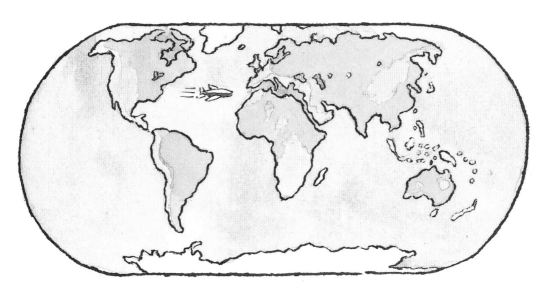

Some parents travel to other countries
to meet their children.

Some parents adopt children when they are babies.

They often meet them for the first time in
the hospital when the baby is born.

Some parents adopt children who are older.

They meet them for the first time in other places.

They might meet at a small home where one or two children are cared for until they are adopted.

Or they might meet at a larger home where many children are cared for until they are adopted.

Children can be adopted at any age!

happy

The day when you
and your parents
get to see each other
for the first time is
very, very special.

sad

shy

There are so many feelings!

If you were adopted as an older child,
you might remember feeling happy, excited,
and a little bit nervous too.
(Even adoptive parents have some of those feelings!)

After all, it's a new beginning
for everybody.

excited

scared

For your parents,
it's one of the happiest days of their lives…

…because soon you will get to go home together.

But first, your adoptive parents have to fill out some very important papers.

There are a lot of papers that go with being adopted!

These are so important because they make your adoption legal.

LEGAL = Just right and permanent. That means for keeps.

Now you are their child and they are your parents.
You are a family!

And now it is time to go home.
This could be a long trip…

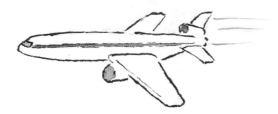

…or a shorter ride.

On the way home, both kids and parents usually have lots of feelings: happy, nervous, excited, curious, and other feelings, too. Older kids might think:

I'm so glad to be going to my new home!

I wonder what my school will be like?

I'm so excited about being adopted!

Will I be happy there?

Will people like me?

Will I miss where I was before?

Are there other adopted kids there?

Can you name some other feelings?

Even babies have feelings.
They know that something has changed
when they are adopted.

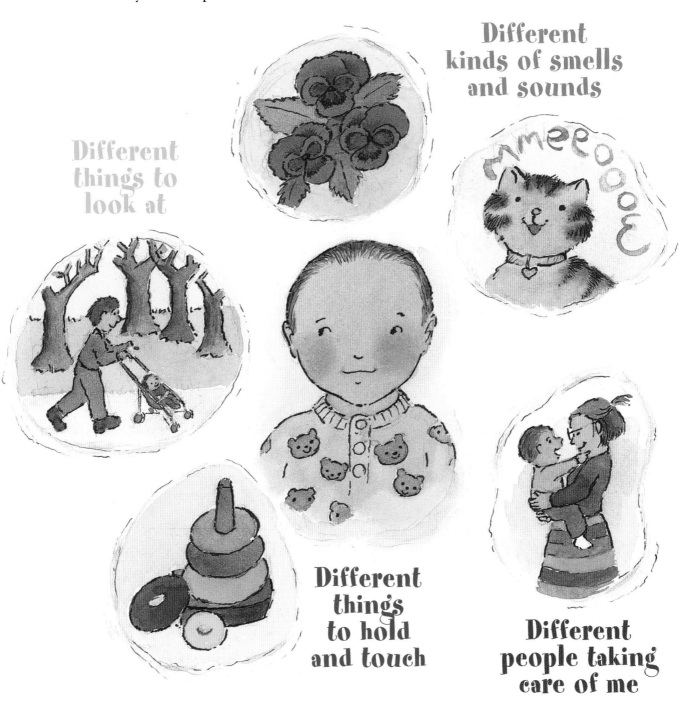

Different
kinds of smells
and sounds

Different
things to
look at

Different
things
to hold
and touch

Different
people taking
care of me

Can you name some other changes?

At your new home,
there are so many things to discover:

A whole
new
house
to get
to know

Your new room

Lots
of new
kids

**Your new
backyard**

SUNNYSIDE
SCHOOL

Your
new
school

**Your new
neighborhood**

So much to get used to
and so hard to get used to so much…

…but pretty exciting too!

There are lots of changes all at once:
new people, new places, new things.

You're in the "getting to know you"
part of being adopted.

Kids can have lots of feelings right about now. These feelings can go up and down and change quickly. It can feel like being on a roller coaster, and that can be pretty confusing.

Babies' feelings go up and down too. They can be quiet, cranky, sad, and happy too. That's because babies also have a "getting to know you" part of being adopted.

Sometimes after the "getting to know you" part of being adopted, kids have even more feelings.

Sometimes they can feel sad when they think about their birth mothers and fathers not being their parents. They even wonder if this happened because of something about them, or if they did something wrong. They may know this isn't true, but they worry about it anyway.

The sad feelings get better when kids remember how much their moms and dads want them and love them. It also helps kids when they remember that their parents think they're great just the way they are.

Sometimes children feel curious
about their birth mother and father.
Kids might wonder:

What did
they look
like?

What did
they like
to do?

Did they
play
soccer
and the
piano
like I do?

How old
were they?

Most moms and dads have never met the birth
parents. But usually they know a little something
about birth moms and dads. Kids can ask their
mom and dad whenever they feel curious.

Sometimes kids who are adopted have special worries.
One big worry that lots of kids have is: "Could I be un-adopted?"

The answer is **NO!**

Remember, your parents love you, and they worked
really hard to make your adoption legal. And that means
Just Right and For Keeps. You are their child forever!

Another worry that lots of adopted children have is:
"Are people I like going to go away?"

Kids have this worry because they already had to say
goodbye to their birth moms and dads, and they are
afraid it could happen again. When kids worry about
this, they are mixing up something that happened
a long time ago with the way things are now.

Remember, what happened before is different
from what is happening from now on.

Sometimes children feel angry.

They might feel angry at their parents just the way all kids do.

They might feel angry that they didn't get to grow up with their birth parents.

Kids also get angry at their adoptive parents to see how much their parents love them. They don't even know they are doing this sometimes! It's like giving their parents a test. The test is, "If you really love me, you'll love me even if I feel angry or misbehave."

Parents always pass this test, of course, because they do love their kids so much.

It is really confusing for both children and parents when they feel angry at each other. But people can feel angry at someone they love.

It helps everyone to know that these feelings happen a lot in all families.

Sometimes children feel different
from other kids because they are adopted.

They might think a lot about whether
they look very different from their parents
and brothers and sisters, or their classmates.

This worry happens even more when children are adopted
from a different country, a different race, or a different culture.
Then some adopted children wonder if they will fit in.

It's normal to have this worry.
The best thing to remember is just to be yourself.

That's what helps all of us like ourselves, feel the best,
and fit in. This works at home, at school, and with our
friends. Once people get to know us, they don't care
whether we're adopted or not.

Q

Some kids worry about what to do if other kids ask,

"Why don't you look like your parents?"

A

The simplest answer is the best:

"Because I'm adopted."

Q

Sometimes adopted children are asked,

"But why were you adopted?"

A

A good answer is,

"Because my mom and dad love me and they wanted me to be in their family."

39

When kids are adopted from another country,
learning about that country can feel good.
It's fun and interesting, and it helps kids feel
proud about all the things that make them special.
You and your family can cook foods from your
first country and learn words
in the country's language.
It's also exciting to read all about
the country and look at pictures
and maps together.
You and your family might even
get to know other children
adopted from there.

Our country is made up of people
from many different countries
and cultures and colors.

And many, many people
are adopted.

People like us because of who we are,
not because of our color,
or what country we come from,
or if we are adopted or not.

And the most important thing to remember is

All families are more the same than they are different.

A family is a family, and families are where children are loved.

Note to Parents

Children are often a source of joy, wonder, and enrichment. Along with vast rewards, raising children—all children—also presents an amazing array of challenges. When adoption is part of a family's history, parents and children alike can expect to face certain challenges that are unique to this profound life experience.

Challenges for Adoptive Parents

Children think about their adoption. Children have interests, concerns, worries, and fantasies about their adoption. This is normal and should be expected, even with the best-adjusted children and regardless of how well the adoption has been explained or how thoroughly the child's feelings about it have been expressed. This is particularly true when children are adopted at a later age, as they bring with them a longer pre-adoption history. It does not signify a problem. It just means that adoption is on their minds.

Children's concerns about being adopted ebb and flow over time. It is vital that parents be open to a child's questions and feelings, regardless of having talked them through before. Questions and feelings take a different form with different life experiences and stressors, as well as at different developmental stages. For example, the wonderings of a four-year-old are not the same as a fourteen-year-old's. In particular, concerns often emerge at these developmental stages:

- the initial phase of adoption (assuming that the child was not adopted as an infant)
- kindergarten, which is always associated with separation issues for children and often includes the challenge of dealing with a larger peer group
- puberty, due to the reemergence of separation issues and the inherent curiosity about sexuality and human reproduction
- mid-adolescence, when dating begins in earnest and teen pregnancy is a possibility (Mid-adolescence is a particularly vulnerable period for children whose birth parents were teenagers themselves.)
- early adulthood, as children are consolidating an adult identity (Adoption is an important and permanent part of their identity. As young adults figure out who they are, they naturally want to know more about their roots, and thus their birth parents.)

All children want to know how they became part of their families. Whether born or adopted into them, children like to hear about their early histories (e.g., pregnancy, pre-adoption, what they were like as babies or younger children, etc.). Frequent conversations handled in a matter-of-fact way about how we all came to be together are essential. When there are non-adopted siblings, try to create parallel descriptions. For example, "Your brother was born in March, and you were adopted in May. You both were born in a hospital. Your brother grew in my tummy; you grew in your birth mom's tummy. And now we are all together."

Children may have feelings about not being a "blood" relative. This is most likely in families where there are non-adopted children, and it can happen despite parents' best efforts. The adopted child *may* think he or she does not have as much of a claim in the family. Also, the adopted child may be distinctively different from all of the biological family members. For example, physical appearance or athletic talents may differ. This occurs most frequently in international or intercultural adoptions. Children will always compare themselves to their siblings, and this is just another variation.

All children struggle at various times with feeling "different." Their struggles may include learning disabilities, attentional problems, developmental delays, and emotional/social difficulties. When adopted children have these problems, their feelings of being different are often intensified by the overlay of their adoptive issues and concerns. The adoption overlay can make managing any common childhood struggle more difficult for the whole family.

Adopted children may continually worry about being abandoned, rejected, "sent back," or "un-adopted." This worry is usually linked to feelings of insecurity. Children may worry that the reason for their original adoption was something lacking in themselves. *(Note: not all children feel this way.)* Parents are often puzzled by these fears, because they have done a good job explaining the permanence of adoption and the reasons for adoption. Even when parents have clearly and lovingly claimed their youngster, children can still worry. Sometimes children act out this worry by misbehaving, often unaware that they are doing it. It's as if they are unconsciously asking, "If I behave really badly, will you send me back?"

This is a love test for parents. Of course children don't want to be sent back; it's their worst fear. Children need to hear that they are adopted forever and will be loved forever. It can take many love tests and explanations before the child fully believes it.

All parents want and need occasional expressions of gratitude and appreciation from their children. When thanks happen (certainly not an everyday occurrence), it's a wonderful feeling, and when they don't, it's disappointing. When one considers how much parents go through in the adoption process—emotionally, logistically, and financially—it is especially stinging when the child appears ungrateful or directly expresses ingratitude. It helps to remember that all children sometimes have trouble expressing their appreciation, even when they are aware of it. Further, as children get older, they often become better able to recognize and express their thankfulness for their parents.

Guidelines for Understanding Your Child's Feelings

All adopted children have fantasies and questions about their birth parents. These can continue throughout development and include specific notions about who the birth parents actually were, what they were like, where they lived, what they looked like, and how old they were. Parents are often unsure how to respond.

In our experience, it is best to give simple and honest explanations and to give children lots of room to express themselves. Don't be alarmed by the fantasies they may articulate, such as, "My dad was a football star" or "My mom was a beautiful ballet dancer." Such fantasies are common. We recommend a reply such as, "I don't know whether your birth dad was a football star. We do know that he did like sports" or "Actually, there was nothing in the papers that said that your birth mom was a dancer, but they did say that she liked reading a lot and was very popular."

Many children, adopted or not, develop fantasy parents. This most commonly occurs around age eight, but with children who are not adopted, parents don't usually hear about such fantasies. In general, these fantasies typically resolve within a year or two when the child makes peace with the glamorous wish and accepts the ordinariness of his or her parents.

Children sometimes ask about going back to their birth parents. Some of this can be a venting of the child's anger or sadness, and sometimes it's just normal curiosity. It's best that parents (1) reassure their children that adoption is forever and (2) encourage their children to talk about their feelings.

This may require directly asking your child about his or her angry, sad, or curious feelings in order to get to the bottom of the reunification fantasy. Reunification fantasies can sometimes reflect a wish to undo the feeling of "original rejection" that may accompany adoption. It can also be linked to a fantasy of trying to fix what they might imagine was wrong in the first place that led to their adoption. Of course, there is nothing that needs fixing. Children are helped when their parents correctly see through their verbalized feelings. Reassure them that they are loved for who they are and that their adoption did not happen because of anything lacking in them.

Adopted children have feelings of sadness, loss, and anger associated with their adoption. It's usually hard for adoptive parents to listen to their children talk about sadness and loss regarding their birth parents, even though such feelings are normal and commonly expressed. Some adopted children wish to have their birth parents be their "real" parents. When children say this, it is important that parents remember they are trying to grapple with possible feelings of rejection by the birth parents and are not repudiating the adoptive parents.

Usually these kinds of comments are a way, albeit not a healthy one, for a child to express anger. When they are angry, all children often say the most hurtful things to their parents. They know how to push our buttons! For adopted children, this can take the form, "You're not my real mom and dad." The best way to handle it is to remember that these comments are common expressions of anger and to help the child understand the feelings and talk about them more directly and constructively.

Children need room and support in order to talk about their feelings and fantasies related to their adoption. It's not always easy for parents to hear their child's thoughts, but children's ultimate adjustment is far better when parents give them clear permission to share anything on their minds. (*Note: be careful that the permission isn't experienced by the child as a demand. Encouraging expression without requiring it is a bit like walking a tightrope!*)

Practical Tips for Parents

Answer a child's questions about the birth parents with simple, honest, and basic information. Explain that it takes a birth mother and a birth father to create a baby. Provide the child with some information about the birth parents, such as physical characteristics and general attributes and interests. Otherwise, the child feels a void and fills in the blanks in ways that may be inaccurate, distorted, and negative. For example, you might tell your daughter that her dad was six feet tall, a good student, liked drama, and had blue eyes and blond hair.

Children may also ask, "Did you know them?" Usually the honest answer is the best one. Thus, you might reply, "No, we never met your birth parents but we can tell you a little bit about them," or "Yes, we met them once and this is what they were like…."

Do not elaborate with any information that might be unnecessarily distressing or unhelpful. For example, a child does not need to know that he or she was conceived under violent circumstances, or that the birth mother was abandoned by the birth father when he found out she was pregnant.

It is helpful for the child to know some specific circumstances of the adoption itself. For example, it would be useful for your son to know that his birth mother was trying to raise him all by herself and knew that she couldn't do the best job of taking care of him. Therefore, she made the decision to place him for adoption.

Your child might ask, "Why did I grow in someone else's tummy?" A good answer might be, "Some really good moms and dads aren't able to be birth mothers and fathers because it's hard for their bodies to make a baby." Another response could be, "Sometimes moms and dads just want to adopt a child because there are so many wonderful children ready to be adopted."

And finally, children often ask, "Will I ever get

to meet my birth mom and dad?" This is not an easy question for many parents. We find a simple answer often works best: "Maybe some day when you are an adult. Some children do and some don't. That's a decision adopted children can make when they grow up."

Use caution when telling children they were "chosen." Adoptive parents are often advised to stress that their child was "chosen" and thus very much wanted. It is good for children to know that they are much wanted, but there can be a downside to overemphasizing being "chosen." It can exacerbate the feelings of differentness that adoptive children sometimes have, and it can also lead the child to feel like an object that was handpicked for the parents. Further, any biological children in the family may feel jealous because they were *not* chosen.

Celebrating just the birthday is best. Adoptive parents are sometimes encouraged to celebrate two special days for their children instead of one; the child's birthday and the adoption day. We generally recommend that only the birthday be celebrated. This is consistent with what families do and thus highlights the child's sameness rather than his or her differentness.

Keep alive the cultural heritage of the children's country of origin when they are adopted internationally. It is both enriching and interesting for all children to know about their ethnic backgrounds. Exposure to another culture is broadening for the entire family and helps the adoptive child feel more at home.

Children appreciate having in their homes objects that are native to their birthplace, such as a piece of pottery, a hand-woven article, or something with the name of the town or country on it. Also, parents might hang a map or a flag from the child's country of origin, read together about the country, and learn about its foods and cooking practices. Eating in local ethnic restaurants is also fun.

Some communities have groups for adoptive children from specific countries. These groups offer children the chance to meet others from their birth country and help them keep their traditions and culture alive. As always, moderation is the key. Overemphasis of cultural differences can lead to feelings of separateness rather than feelings of pride and connectedness. Each child's balance point is different, requiring parental sensitivity and awareness.

Most children are delighted when parents keep a scrapbook specifically for them. Fill the scrapbook with all the usual photos and mementos that children and families accumulate together and that portray their life as a family. For adoptive children, the book could also include:
- the first photos of the child that are available (including pre-adoption)
- photos of the birthplace and immediate surrounding environment (hospital, neighborhood, foster parents, and so forth, as appropriate)
- photos of the country of origin, or city, state, or region of this country. A child born in China could find it useful to see pictures of where she was born and where she lived prior to being adopted, as well as written information about her place of origin—even a tourist pamphlet. There is a lot of history that you aren't able to give an adopted child, so it is very important to give those things that you do have from her pre-adoption life.

Adopted children bring many joys to their families. They also bring, as do all children, moments of worry and frustration. By continually conveying your ongoing availability and willingness to talk about the many feelings that arise as they grow up, you will find the journey easier, richer, and more beneficial for everyone.

About the Authors

Marc Nemiroff, Ph.D., serves on the core faculty of the Washington School of Psychiatry's Infant and Young Children Mental Health Training Program and the clinical faculty of George Washington University's Doctor of Psychology program. He is also an Affiliate Member of the Baltimore-District of Columbia Society for Psychoanalysis, and he maintains a private practice for the treatment of children in Potomac, Maryland.

Jane Annunziata, Psy.D., is a clinical psychologist with a private practice specializing in children and families in McLean, Virginia. She serves on the clinical faculty of George Washington University's Doctor of Psychology program. As a writer, she has contributed parent guidance sections to many children's books on such varied topics as shyness, parental depression, ambivalence, touching and boundaries, and a new baby in the family.

Dr. Nemiroff and Dr. Annunziata are the authors of *Sex & Babies: First Facts*, *A Child's First Book About Play Therapy*, *Help Is on the Way: A Child's Book About ADD*, and *Why Am I an Only Child? All About Adoption* is their fifth book together.

About the Illustrator

Carol Koeller is the illustrator of *Mom, Dad, Come Back Soon*, as well as several educational books. Her expressive characters also appear in children's magazines and on greeting cards. She grew up on the East Coast, spent ten years in California, and then settled in Chicago, where she now lives with her husband, two daughters, and various pets. *All About Adoption* is her second picture book for Magination Press.